Ten Tiny Aliens
and the
Great Big Pet Disaster

Debbie White

Illustrated by
Aleksei Bitskoff

OXFORD
UNIVERSITY PRESS

OXFORD
UNIVERSITY PRESS

Great Clarendon Street, Oxford, OX2 6DP,
United Kingdom

Oxford University Press is a department of the University of Oxford.
It furthers the University's objective of excellence in research, scholarship,
and education by publishing worldwide. Oxford is a registered trade mark of
Oxford University Press in the UK and in certain other countries

Text © Debbie White 2017

Illustrations © Aleksei Bitskoff 2017

The moral rights of the author have been asserted

First published 2017

All rights reserved. No part of this publication may be reproduced, stored
in a retrieval system, or transmitted, in any form or by any means, without
the prior permission in writing of Oxford University Press, or as expressly
permitted by law, by licence or under terms agreed with the appropriate
reprographics rights organization. Enquiries concerning reproduction outside
the scope of the above should be sent to the Rights Department, Oxford
University Press, at the address above.

You must not circulate this work in any other form
and you must impose this same condition on any acquirer

British Library Cataloguing in Publication Data
Data available

978-0-19-837752-8

7 9 10 8 6

Paper used in the production of this book is a natural, recyclable product
made from wood grown in sustainable forests. The manufacturing process
conforms to the environmental regulations of the country of origin.

Printed in China

Acknowledgements
Inside cover notes written by Gill Howell
Author photograph by Michael Stockton Photography

Contents

1 Always Read the Label 5
2 What Can Go Wrong *This* Time? 13
3 The Perfect Pet? 23
4 Shrinking Eric 33
5 Eric Fits In 40
6 A Big Problem 48
About the author 64

Chapter 1
Always Read the Label

This is the faraway planet, Zap. It looks a bit like Earth. Except the rivers and seas are orange and the mountains are pink.

It's home to the Teeny Tiny Aliens, who are just like us. Except they only have three fingers on each hand and three toes on each foot … and they are purple. And instead of hair, they have lovely wavy tentacles (a bit like teeny tiny elephant trunks).

This is Chief Big Teeny Tiny. He's in charge. He wears a teeny tiny T-shirt, which says CHIEF on it in big letters.

These are the Chief's little cousins, Itsy Teeny Tiny and Weeny Teeny Tiny. The Chief thinks they should wear T-shirts that say TROUBLE.

Itsy and Weeny don't mean to upset the Chief. They want to *help* him but, somehow, things always go wrong. Like the time the Chief was poorly with the spiffle spots (itchy spots that glow in the dark and change colour).

"He needs cheering up," said Itsy. "Having spiffle spots is no fun at all."

"Let's look up spiffle spots on the computer and see what will help," said Weeny.

So that night, Itsy and Weeny filled the Chief's bubble tub with lots of nice, hot, orange water and an *enormous* glug of Womple Juice.

"You look tired," said Weeny to the Chief.

"Warm bubbly water with Womple Juice will make you feel *much* better," said Itsy. "And why not put in some of your favourite Pongee Crystals?"

"What a lovely idea," said the Chief, getting into his bubble tub and pressing the bubble button.

"Aaah, bliss," he said. "Well done, Itsy and Weeny. My spiffle spots have stopped itching."

Itsy and Weeny were very pleased.

"Now for those Pongee Crystals," said the Chief, sprinkling them on to the bubbly water.

The water got bubblier …

and bubblier …

and bubblier.

Oops!

The bubbles rose up and covered the Chief. They filled the bubble tub. Then the whole room was full of bubbles … and the bubbles were heading out of the door. So were Itsy and Weeny. They'd just remembered what the *Monster Guide to Alien Spots* had said about mixing Womple Juice with Pongee Crystals …

DON'T!

"Come back, you pesky teeny tinies!" shouted the Chief as he jumped out of the bubble tub ... and slipped right over. Crash! Bang! Ouch!

Poor Chief Big Teeny Tiny. He'd banged his elbow, hurt his bottom and his tentacles were bruised black and blue. He was *very* cross.

"Just wait until I catch up with you, Itsy and Weeny!"

An hour later, Itsy and Weeny were standing in front of Chief Big Teeny Tiny.

"We're really, really sorry, aren't we, Weeny?" said Itsy.

"Really, really sorry," said Weeny.

"You're always sorry!" bellowed the Chief. "Then you do something silly again! This time, take your Teeny Tiny Submarine to the bottom of the Teeny Tiny Sea for a whole week," said the Chief. "And *next* time you do something silly, I'm going to banish you from Zap!"

Chapter 2
What Can Go Wrong This Time?

Itsy and Weeny didn't enjoy being at the bottom of the Teeny Tiny Sea. It was dark down there, and very boring.

Except on the *very last* day, when a Great Green Slurp Bubbler sneaked up and tried to swallow their Teeny Tiny Submarine. Luckily, Itsy and Weeny saw it just in time!

Phew! They'd escaped being slurped *and* they were back in time for Chief Big Teeny Tiny's birthday party.

"I've got this amazing idea for his birthday present. The Chief's been saying for ages that he wants a pet," said Weeny.

"Let's get him two!" said Itsy.

So Itsy and Weeny went off and bought a pair of lovely little bug-eyed ziplets (plus zip-basket).

Then they went to the Teeny Tiny Bakery and ordered the Chief a special birthday cake. It had a hole cut out of the middle (for the ziplets to hide in). It had a pop-off lid (so the ziplets could pop up out of the cake) *and* it was covered in green slime icing. Yummy!

"He'll be so excited when he sees the ziplets jump out of the cake," said Itsy.

"Easy peasy womple squeezy. One, two, three, ta-dah!" said Weeny.

"What on Zap can go wrong *this* time?" said Itsy.

The Chief's birthday party started well. DJ Teeny Tiny Smalls was playing the Chief's favourite teeny tiny music tracks.

There were games (hunt the tromble, pin the tail on the wobblebuck and tentacle braiding).

There were scrumptious things to eat. Then finally it was time for Itsy and Weeny to bring in the cake.

The Chief looked very pleased when he saw it. "Green slime icing, my favourite! Thank you," he said.

"But this is the best bit," said Weeny.

"One, two, three!" shouted Itsy, popping the lid off the cake.

Well, it is true that ziplets make lovely pets … as long as they don't eat green slime icing. All that sugar makes them go *super* zippy.

Oops!

Zipzipzipzipzipzip!

The ziplets took off like rockets.

Green slime icing was flying everywhere (and mostly landing on the Chief). Chief Big Teeny Tiny looked like something from the bottom of a big green slimy pond.

"Catch those ziplets, Itsy and Weeny, then come and see me!" shouted the Chief. My word, the Chief was very angry.

Poor Itsy and Weeny. They sat in the middle of the floor and watched the ziplets zipping everywhere. The ziplets were moving so fast they were just a blur.

"We'll never catch them," said Weeny. "They're much too zippy."

But luckily, after a bit, the ziplets ran out of zip. They fell fast asleep in a corner, snoring loudly. Phew! Itsy and Weeny quickly popped them in the zip-basket.

Then they went to say sorry to Chief Big Teeny Tiny.

"We thought you'd be pleased with your present," said Weeny.

"You said you wanted a pet!" said Itsy.

"We didn't know what would happen," said Itsy and Weeny together.

"You never do! I've had enough," said the Chief. "You're banished. Take your Teeny Tiny Spaceship and leave Zap at once. And take those ziplets with you! I want a proper pet, not two annoying little fuzz balls!"

Chapter 3
The Perfect Pet?

Soon poor Weeny and Itsy (and the ziplets) were drifting out in space in their Teeny Tiny Spaceship.

"I'm so miserable. Look, my skin has lost its purple glow! I just want to go home," said Itsy.

Poor Itsy did look very unhappy.

"Don't worry, I've got an ace idea," said Weeny. "Why don't we find Chief Big Teeny Tiny a pet so amazing he'll forgive us and let us go home?"

"Good thinking," said Itsy, brightening up. "Let's look up the *Teeny Tiny Monster Guide to Pets of the Universe*."

Weeny thought the Five-Horned Plip Monster from the planet Plip looked awesome.

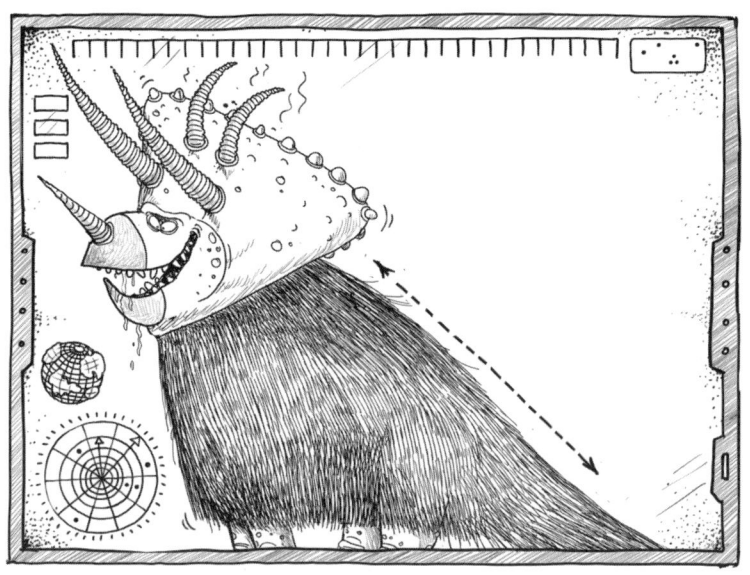

Weeny read the description. "Must have a good supply of its favourite food: Teeny Tiny Aliens."

Oops!

"Well, how about the Bat-Eared Gargler from the planet Gargle?" said Itsy.

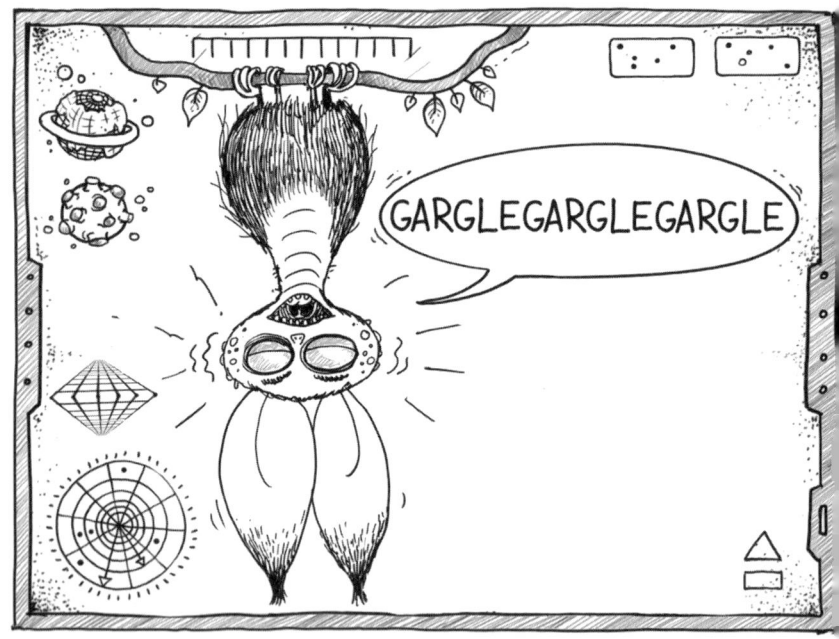

"When asleep, the Bat-Eared Gargler makes a loud gargling noise. This causes its owners to go deaf!" Weeny read.

Oops! Chief Big Teeny Tiny wouldn't be happy about that.

Then, just as Itsy and Weeny were starting to feel glum, a pet from the planet Earth popped up on screen.

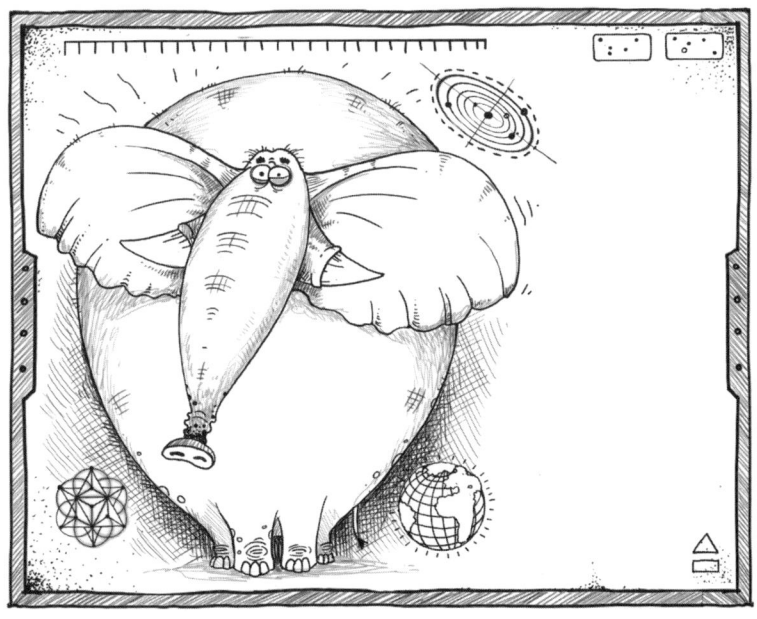

Itsy and Weeny read the description together. "This pet makes a wonderful friend. It is very intelligent and gentle. It can carry its owner long distances on its back."

Hurray!

Itsy and Weeny tapped 'How do we get to Earth?' into the spaceship's Teeny Tiny Computer.

Then they set off, not even stopping for breakfast.

At 12 noon, they landed safely on planet Earth.

Ping! The spaceship door opened and Itsy and Weeny (and the ziplets) popped out into a forest of green.

"Zapping Zoozies!" said Weeny. "It's going to be hard to spot our pet in here!"

"Don't worry," said Itsy, "I've got a picture of it. *And* we can use our Teeny Tiny Tracking Device."

So off they set.

They swished their way through the green forest. They hid from fearsome monsters with scary pincers and lots of legs. At last the Teeny Tiny Tracking Device said: "You have reached your pet."

Itsy and Weeny walked around and around in circles looking for it.

"Where is it?" said Weeny, giving the tracking device a good hard thump.

Poor Teeny Tinies, they *were* worn out.

"Let's take a teeny tiny nap," said Itsy, "and then carry on looking."

"Good idea," said Weeny.

They had just settled down for a teeny tiny snooze when the ground started shaking. What on Earth was happening?

Itsy and Weeny opened their eyes and looked up …

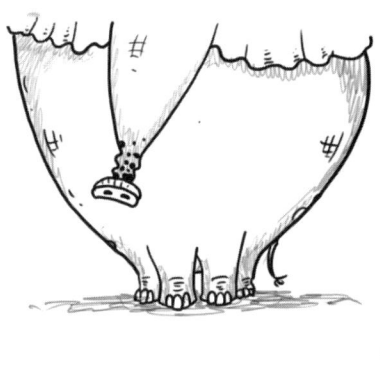

and up …

and up.

Itsy looked down at the picture of the pet on the screen.

Oops!

"I think we've found our pet," said Itsy.

"But it's the size of our planet!" squeaked Weeny.

Chapter 4
Shrinking Eric

Itsy looked up at the giant pet. "Perhaps," said Itsy, "we'd better *ask* it if it would like to go to Zap."

"You're right," said Weeny. "It's only polite, after all."

So Itsy got out the Teeny Tiny Translator and Megaphone.

"We are Itsy and Weeny Teeny Tiny from the planet Zap. Would you like to travel home with us in our spaceship?"

"Pleased to meet you, Itsy and Weeny. My name is Eric. I've always wanted to meet some Teeny Tiny Aliens and visit another planet," he said.

What luck!

So Itsy and Weeny got out their Teeny Tiny Collapsible Measuring Device and, with the help of the ziplets, they measured Eric. Then they measured their Teeny Tiny Spaceship.

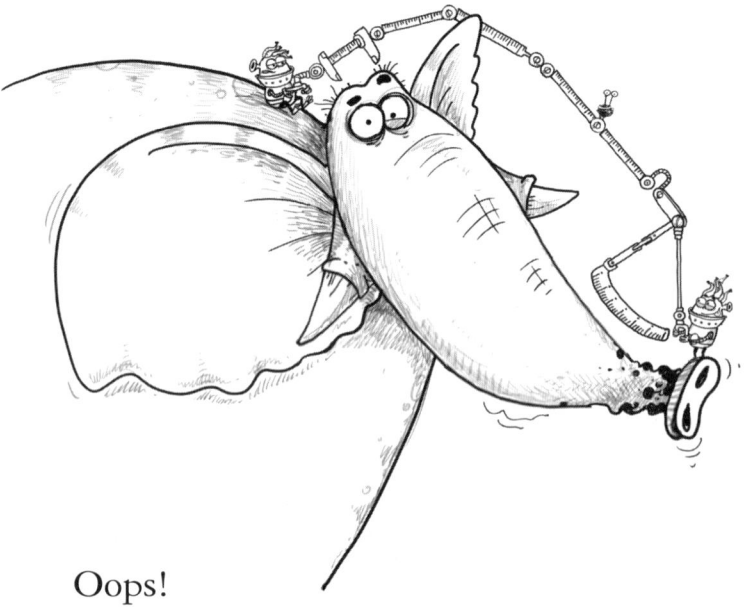

Oops!
Eric would never fit inside.

"Perhaps we can tie him on top of our spaceship?" said Weeny.

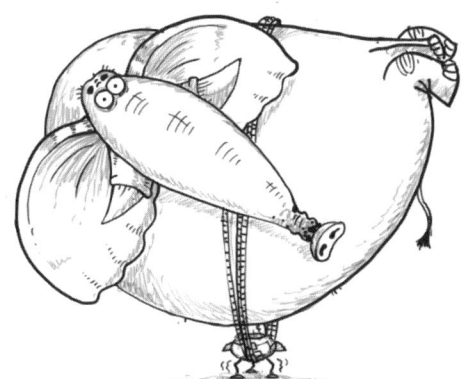

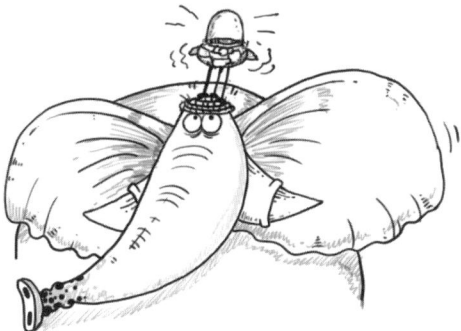

"Or tie him underneath?" said Itsy.

"We'll just have to use the Teeny Tiny Shrink-n-Grow Machine on Eric," said Weeny, "and hope nothing goes wrong *this* time."

You see, the last time they used the Shrink-n-Grow, they shrunk the Chief's *house* by mistake.

What luck the Chief hadn't been in it!

The Chief had banned them from using the Shrink-n-Grow Machine ever again.

But Eric was willing to give it a go. He really, *really* wanted to travel to another planet.

So Itsy and Weeny used the Shrink-n-Grow Machine on Eric. Luckily, he came out just the right size to fit inside the Teeny Tiny Spaceship.

Phew! Itsy and Weeny and Eric (and the ziplets) took off for the planet Zap.

Eric was very excited to see Earth from high above. "Woo-hoo!"

When they landed on Zap, Chief Big Teeny Tiny said, "Itsy and Weeny, I've missed you. I forgive you for hiding those ziplets in my birthday cake. Now show me what you've brought back from planet Earth."

The Chief was very excited. He'd never seen an Eric before and he was very keen to meet one. Luckily for Itsy and Weeny, Eric and the Chief got on *very* well.

"We're going to be best friends," said the Chief.

"It's like I've known you forever," said Eric.

"My great-great-great-great-great-great-great-great-great-great grandmother left Zap to look for new planets," said the Chief. "I know she visited Earth many Zap moons ago. You and I might be related, Eric!" said the Chief.

Eric was thrilled to think he might be part Teeny Tiny Alien!

Things were going so well …

Chapter 5
Eric Fits In

The Chief invited Eric to stay at his new house.

"Make yourself at home," he said.

Eric was very impressed. He'd never seen a house before, let alone a Teeny Tiny Alien one.

"This is the teeny tiny kitchen," said the Chief. "I expect you're hungry after your trip. What do Erics eat? How about a Zap Burger and some nice blue leaves?"

Eric wasn't sure about the burger, but he tried the leaves. If he closed his eyes, they tasted just like Earth ones. Yummy. Eric finished off all the leaves and looked around for some more. The Chief had some nice-looking ones growing on his windowsill. Eric ate those as well.

"...is is the teeny tiny bubble tub ...er room," said the Chief.

...wasn't sure he liked the look of t... bubble tub. The water looked very soapy. He took a drink. Yuk – it tasted horrid!

But the 'warm rain coming down out of the sky' thing looked fun. Eric stepped in. Soon he was squirting water everywhere and singing very loudly.

It was nearly bedtime before the Chief could get Eric out of the shower.

"And this is where you can sleep," said the Chief. "Itsy and Weeny and the ziplets will keep you company. You can have a teeny tiny sleepover. That will be fun, won't it?"

Eric had never seen a teeny tiny bed before. On Earth, he slept on a fresh pile of leaves ... then ate them for breakfast the next morning.

He jumped on the bed. It was very springy. Boing! Boing! Boing! Itsy and Weeny jumped on too. So did the ziplets. Even the Chief had a go.

Things were going brilliantly!

The next day, the Chief took Eric and Itsy and Weeny (and the ziplets) out in the Big Zapmobile. And everywhere they went, Teeny Tinies came out to cheer and wave. They'd never seen an Eric before.

That evening Eric, Chief Big Teeny Tiny and Itsy and Weeny (and the ziplets) were on the Teeny Tiny TV news.

"Phew," thought Itsy and Weeny. The Chief wouldn't banish them *ever* again, would he? Not now they were Teeny Tiny TV stars.

Chapter 6
A Big Problem

Itsy and Weeny were feeling cheerful. Days and *days* had gone by and the Chief hadn't lost his temper once! In fact, he seemed to be in a very good mood. Even when Eric ate all the plants in the Chief's teeny tiny garden, he'd just smiled and said, "What luck! Now I don't need to do any gardening."

And when Eric drank all the water from the Chief's garden pond he'd said, "What luck! The pool needed cleaning out anyway."

But the Chief did get a *teeny tiny* bit cross when Eric got stuck in the front seat of the Zapmobile. It took the Chief, Itsy *and* Weeny ages to pull him out.

"You're getting fat, Eric," the Chief said.

Poor Eric. It wasn't *his* fault. He seemed to be very hungry these days. It was getting to be a tight squeeze in the shower too. And only yesterday he'd jumped on the bed and broken it! What was going on?

Itsy and Weeny had an idea of what the problem might be. They weren't going to tell anyone, though. Not yet, anyway. Not until things got *really* bad and there were big problems with Eric.

"We shrank Eric with the Shrink-n-Grow machine, but only for a little while. Soon he'll be back to his *real* size," said Weeny.

"The size of our planet," said Itsy.

"Yes. Then the Chief will be really, *really* mad. This time, we might get banished for good," said Weeny.

Chief Big Teeny Tiny stopped being cheerful when Eric accidentally sat on the Zapmobile and squashed it flat. He started to look cross when Eric tried to get through the front door of the house ... and left a great big Eric-shaped hole in the wall.

But he looked very, *very* cross indeed when Eric went swimming in the Teeny Tiny Sea and whooshed so much water out there was hardly any left!

"Right, you pesky Teeny Tinies!" said the Chief. "Tell me what's going on."

"It's not Eric's fault. We had to use the Shrink-n-Grow machine to make him fit in the Teeny Tiny Spaceship. He was quite big, you see," said Itsy.

Oops!

They hadn't told the Chief about the shrinking.

"*How* big was Eric before you shrank him?" the Chief asked.

"Quite big," said Itsy.

"Bigger than he is now," said Weeny.

The Chief gave them a fierce stare.

"About the size of our planet," said Itsy in a very squeaky voice.

The Chief didn't speak for quite a long time. He'd gone a deep purple colour, and he looked like he might explode.

"Right, well, you'll have to shrink him again. I'm very fond of Eric, so I hope nothing goes wrong this time. Then you must take him straight back to his home planet. Maybe you two could stay on Earth with Eric. How would you like that?"

Itsy and Weeny didn't want to stay on Earth. They loved Zap. They didn't want to use the Shrink-n-Grow machine on Eric, either. Supposing this time they shrank him too much?

But Eric was very brave. He gave Itsy and Weeny a hug with his trunk.

"Do it! I've had a brilliant time on Zap," he said, "but I *really* miss Earth. I want to go home and see my family."

So they zapped Eric and held their breath.

Phew! Eric shrank to a perfect teeny tiny size!

Soon Itsy and Weeny and Eric (and the ziplets) landed back on Earth. They stepped out into the forest of green.

"I've had a brilliant time being small," Eric said, looking around. "But I'd really like to be big now, before something eats me!"

Itsy and Weeny looked at the Shrink-n-Grow Machine.

"We've never actually *grown* anything before, Eric."

"Do it!" said Eric, giving them a big smile.

So Itsy and Weeny zapped Eric with the Shrink-n-Grow machine.

What luck! Now Eric was a proper-sized elephant again.

"If only we could go back home to Zap," said Itsy.

"We can't. The Chief was very cross," said Weeny.

"Crosser than he's ever been before," said Itsy.

"What if we promise *never* to do anything silly *ever* again?" said Weeny.

"And *mean* it this time," said Itsy.

Eric shook his head and sighed. He loved Itsy and Weeny. He wanted them to be happy ... on Zap.

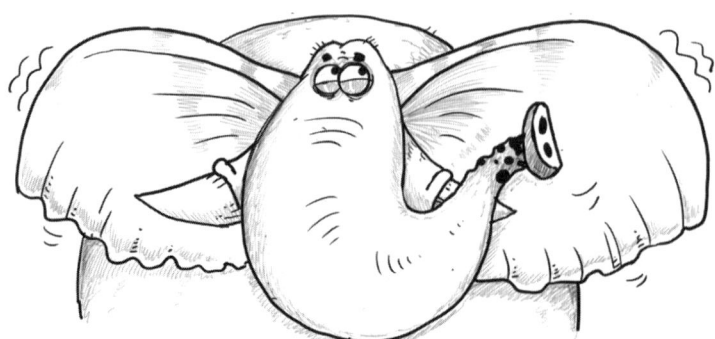

Just then, Itsy's Teeny Tiny Space Phone pinged. Itsy and Weeny held their breath. What was the Chief going to say?

"Grrrr! You two make me so angry," he said, "but you *are* family and I miss you. So you can come home … but leave that pesky Shrink-n-Grow machine behind with Eric!"

So Itsy and Weeny gave Eric the
Shrink-n-Grow Machine.

"Look after it, won't
you?" said Weeny.

"Promise you won't
forget us!" said Itsy.

"Elephants never
forget," said Eric, "and
the Shrink-n-Grow is quite
safe with me."

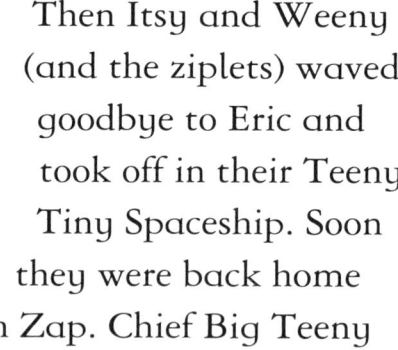

Then Itsy and Weeny
(and the ziplets) waved
goodbye to Eric and
took off in their Teeny
Tiny Spaceship. Soon
they were back home
on Zap. Chief Big Teeny
Tiny was very pleased to see them and
they all had a *great* big hug.

Itsy and Weeny (and the ziplets) were happy. The Chief was smiling and happy. Itsy and Weeny had promised not to be silly ever again ... and the Shrink-n-Grow Machine was far, far away!

"I expect Eric is happy too, now he's back safely on Earth," said Itsy.

"I bet he's having a nice quiet little nap right this minute," said Weeny.

"After all his exciting adventures," said the Chief.

Oops!

About the author

I have two grown-up sons (who were just like Itsy and Weeny) and a very old cat called Martha.

Where did the idea for *Teeny Tiny Aliens and the Great Big Pet Disaster* come from? A very long time ago when I was a little girl, I watched a film about aliens making contact with us on Earth. The last shot of the film showed an alien spaceship landing ... and being crushed under someone's foot! You see, the aliens were very, *very* small. What a great idea – teeny tiny aliens!